bugs

This edition published by Fog City Press
Conceived and produced by Weldon Owen Pty Ltd
61 Victoria Street, McMahons Point
Sydney, NSW 2060, Australia

Copyright © 2008 Weldon Owen Pty Ltd

Group Chief Executive Officer John Owen
President and Chief Executive Officer Terry Newell
Publisher Sheena Coupe
Creative Director Sue Burk
Vice President, International Sales Stuart Laurence
Vice President, Sales and New Business Development Amy Kaneko
Vice President, Sales: Asia and Latin America Dawn Low
Administrator, International Sales Kristine Ravn
Publishing Coordinator Mike Crowton

Consultant Editor Denise Ryan
Managing Editor Jessica Cox
Editor Helen Flint
Designer Gabrielle Green

ISBN: 978-1-74089-663-4

Color reproduction by SC (Sang Choy) International Pte Ltd
Printed by SNP Leefung Printers Ltd
Manufactured in China

10 9 8 7 6 5 4 3

A WELDON OWEN PRODUCTION

my first

encyclopedia of

bugs

Helen Flint

FOG CITY PRESS

Redback spider

Cockroaches

Dragonfly

contents

What is a bug?

Over three-quarters of all living creatures on Earth are bugs. Some have long legs, others have thin bodies, and many have wings. All bugs have a hard outer shell to protect them, and legs with joints. They live all around the world.

Wasp

Dragonfly

Caterpillars

Fly

Spider

SHAKE A LEG

Scorpions, ticks, centipedes, and spiders are not insects, but they are still called bugs. Insects have six legs, but scorpions, ticks, and spiders have eight legs. Centipedes can have as many as 400 legs!

Scorpion

Tick

Centipede

Cockchafer
beetle

Locust

Butterfly

On the move

Insects move in all sorts of ways. Butterflies fly through the air with wings. Caterpillars walk on their legs. Locusts leap on their strong back legs.

Sand wasp

One in every four creatures on Earth is a beetle.

Cicada

Ladybug

Bush cricket

Insects

There are more insects in the world than any other kind of animal. They all have six legs and a body made up of three parts. Insects have a hard shell on the outside that protects the body and forms an external skeleton.

Brain

Antenna
Insects use antennae to feel, smell, and hear.

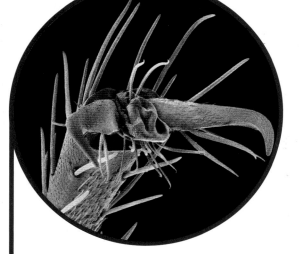

Eye
Insect eyes are made up of many tiny eyes.

Tongue
Bees use their long tongues to suck up nectar.

Most insects have claws on the end of each leg. These help them to cling to different surfaces.

Breathing holes
Insects breathe through holes on the sides of their body.

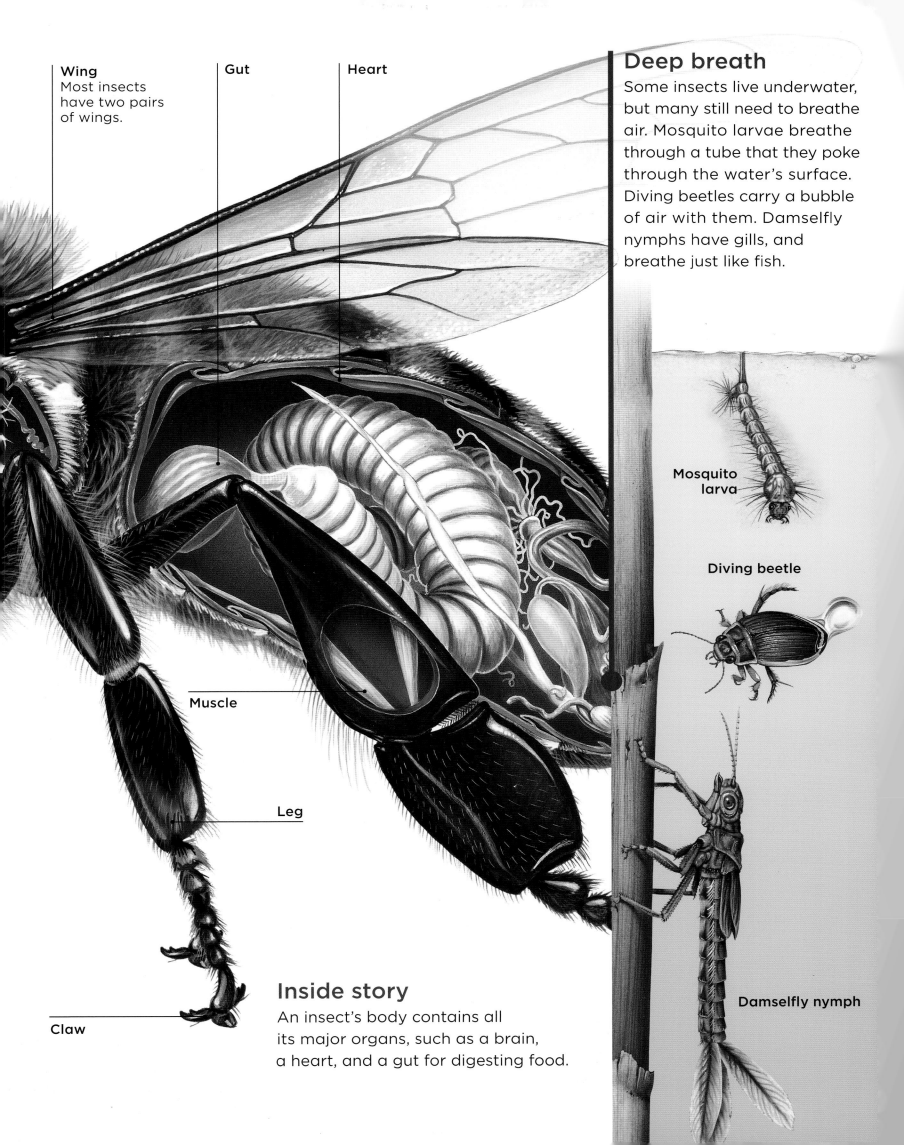

Wing
Most insects
have two pairs
of wings.

Gut

Heart

Deep breath

Some insects live underwater,
but many still need to breathe
air. Mosquito larvae breathe
through a tube that they poke
through the water's surface.
Diving beetles carry a bubble
of air with them. Damselfly
nymphs have gills, and
breathe just like fish.

Mosquito
larva

Diving beetle

Damselfly nymph

Muscle

Leg

Claw

Inside story

An insect's body contains all
its major organs, such as a brain,
a heart, and a gut for digesting food.

Crickets and cockroaches

Crickets and grasshoppers have strong back legs, which they use to leap high into the air. Cockroaches cannot jump. They scuttle about quickly on their legs. They can go for months without food, and can survive in places where no other insect could live.

Field cricket

Green banana roach

Little roach

The tiny ant cockroach is the smallest in the world. It is only as long as a grain of rice.

German cockroach

Ant cockroach

Madagascan hissing cockroach

A cockroach will eat cardboard if there is no other food around.

Up and away

Grasshoppers can jump great distances.
They flick their back legs backward,
to push themselves into the air.
Once up, they use their wings to fly.

Antenna

Leg muscles
Grasshoppers
have strong
leg muscles.

The largest
cockroach is the
giant cockroach.
It is 3 inches
(7.5 cm) long.

DIFFERENT JOBS

Grasshoppers come out during
the day. They have big eyes
to see the world around them.
Cockroaches come out only
at night. They use their long
antennae to find food and
keep safe from danger.

Cockroach

Grasshopper

True bugs

We call many small creatures "bugs," but bugs are actually a special group of insects. They all have long, thin mouths that they use like straws to suck up food. Some bugs use this special mouth to kill and eat other animals. Other bugs feed on plants.

Big mouth

The mouth of the assassin bug is long and sharp. It uses it to stab its victim. It then sucks up the juices inside.

Stabbing mouth

Water scorpion

Flower food

This jester bug sucks up nectar from flowers with its long mouth.

Stink bugs give off a terrible smell when they are threatened. This is to scare away attackers.

Underwater

Ponds are home to many different kinds of bugs. Some live under the water, and others live on the surface. All hunt for food with their long needle-like mouths.

Giant water bugs are so huge they can catch fish.

Water strider

Water boatman

Beetles

There are more than 400,000 kinds of beetles in the world. Beetles have strong front wings, which they use to cover their delicate back wings. This hard covering also keeps them safe from other animals that would like to eat them.

Female beetle

Big fight

Male Hercules beetles use their large horns to fight each other for a female beetle. For their size, Hercules beetles are the strongest creatures on Earth.

Fireflies are actually beetles, not flies.

Ladybugs

Ladybugs are brightly colored to warn other animals that they taste bad.

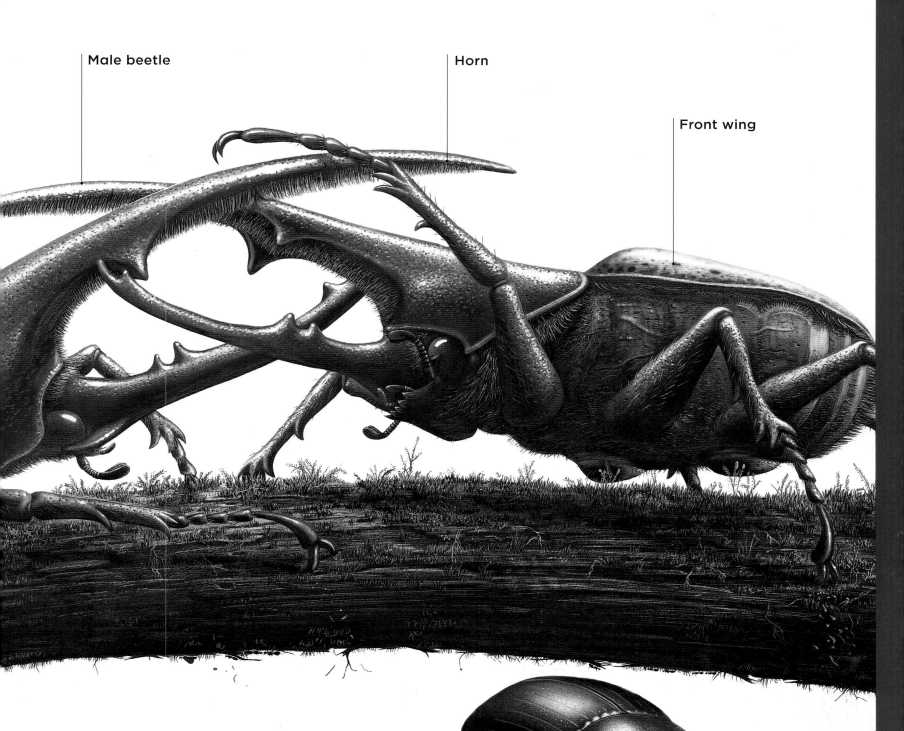

Male beetle

Horn

Front wing

Roll up!

Dung beetles roll animal dung into balls. The female beetle lays her eggs in the dung. When the young are born, they will eat their way out of it.

Dung beetles

Flies and dragonflies

Flies and dragonflies are both good at flying. Flies use one pair of wings to fly. Some flies eat insects, while others feed on rotting meat and plants. Dragonflies have two pairs of wings. They eat insects, such as mosquitoes.

Young flies are called maggots. They are blind and have no legs.

House flies have sticky feet. This is why they can walk on the ceiling.

Hairy bee fly
This fly sticks its long, thin mouth into flowers to get the nectar inside.

FOOD FOR FLIES

All flies eat liquid food. They can make a meal out of almost anything.

House flies
These flies pour their acid saliva onto food to turn it into liquid, before slurping it up.

Fruit flies
These flies eat the juices from rotting fruit.

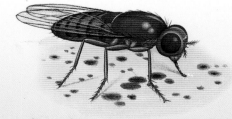

Mosquitoes
These small flies feed on blood.

Eye

Wing
Dragonflies have
two pairs of wings.

Leg

Many eyes

A dragonfly's eye is made up
of thousands of smaller eyes.
A dragonfly can see in all
directions at the same time.

Hover flies

These are the
only flies that can
hover in midair.

Wings
Flies have one
pair of wings.

Butterflies and moths

Butterflies and moths have two pairs of wings, and a pair of long, thin antennae sprouting from their heads. They use their antennae to find food and a partner. Butterflies come out only during the day. Moths usually come out at night.

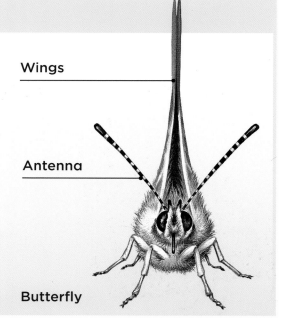

Colorful creatures

Butterflies and moths come in many colors and patterns. Their colors often match the flowers they live on.

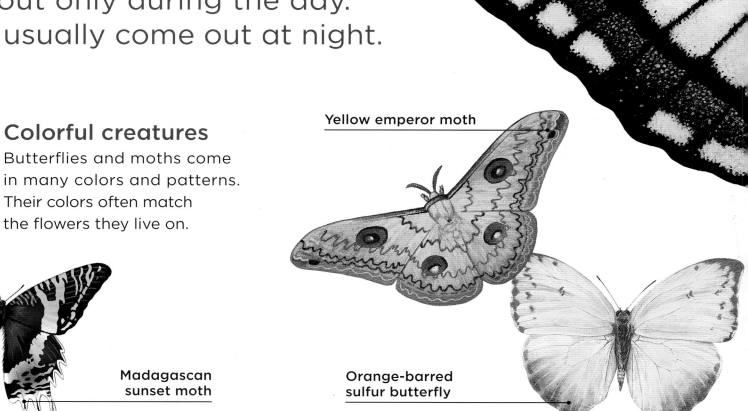

Yellow emperor moth

Madagascan sunset moth

Orange-barred sulfur butterfly

SPOT THE DIFFERENCE

You can tell the difference between a moth and a butterfly by looking at their wings and antennae. Butterflies hold their wings together when they rest. Moths hold them flat. Butterflies have club-shaped antennae. Moths have feathery or plain antennae.

Wing

Antenna

Moth

Wings

Antenna

Butterfly

Swallowtail butterfly

Cabbage
white butterfly

Dinnertime
Butterflies and moths
feed on nectar from
flowers. They use their
curly tongue to eat.

Eighty-eight
butterfly

Bees and wasps

Bees and wasps are different from most other insects because they all have thin waists. Most types of bees and wasps live in groups. Together, they build nests, where they raise their young and store food.

Swarming bees

Bee houses
Bees live in nests called hives. The hives are made of wax. The bees use the hives to store honey and look after their young.

STINGERS

Most bees and wasps have yellow and black stripes. They can sting to defend themselves or their nests. Honeybees die after they have stung once, but most wasps can sting over and over again.

Honeybee

European wasp

Stinger

Male bee

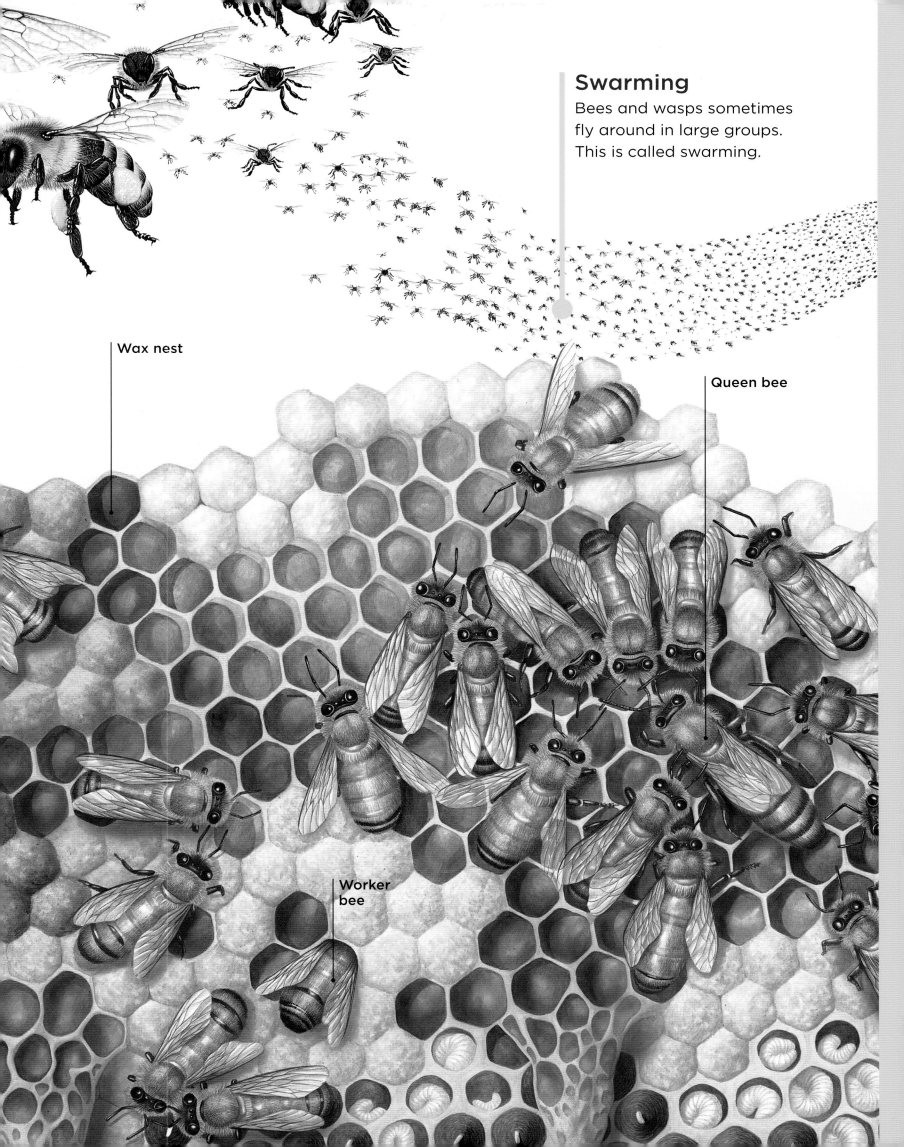

Swarming

Bees and wasps sometimes fly around in large groups. This is called swarming.

Wax nest

Queen bee

Worker bee

Ants

Most ants live and travel in large groups. They build nests that can be underground, in plants, or even up trees. Ant groups are made up of at least two types of ant—the worker ants and the queen ant. The single queen ant produces all the baby ants for the group.

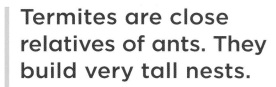

Termites are close relatives of ants. They build very tall nests.

MEETING

When two ants meet, they use their antennae to smell each other. That way, they can find out if they are from the same family.

Cutting leaves

Leaf-cutter ants feed on a special type of fungus that grows on leaves. Worker ants chop the leaves into small pieces. They then carry them back to the nest to be prepared for eating.

Same family, different jobs

Queen ant
She lays all eggs for the nest.

Soldier ants
They protect the nest.

Male ants
They mate with the queen ant.

Worker ants
They collect food.

Ants can live in groups as large as 300 million!

Flying high

Flying is a great way for an insect to get about. It helps it find a new place to live, food to eat, and a new mate to start a family. Flying also helps it to get away from danger quickly. Most insects fly by themselves. Others fly in large groups called swarms.

KINDS OF WINGS

Every kind of insect has a unique set of wings.

Fly

Moth

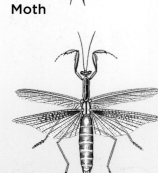

Mantis

A dragonfly can move as fast as an express train.

Head spin

This flea beetle does not fly, but it jumps far through the air. It spins over and over as it goes.

Up and down

This deerfly tilts its wings, and beats them up and down to fly through the air.

Front wing

Back wing

Front wing

Back wing

Taking off!

Ladybugs hide their back wings underneath their hard front wings. When they take off, their wings open out.

Insect world

It is important for insects to know what is going on around them. Just like us, they do this by sight, smell, touch, taste, and sound. Some insects have developed senses that are much stronger than those of humans.

Super sight
This horsefly's eyes are made up of thousands of smaller eyes, called eyelets.

What a human sees   **What a bee sees**

Special sight
Bees see differently from humans. This helps them to see which flowers will have pollen to eat.

Weird ears
Grasshoppers call to each other by rubbing their back legs against their wings. They hear these calls through special "ears" on their abdomens.

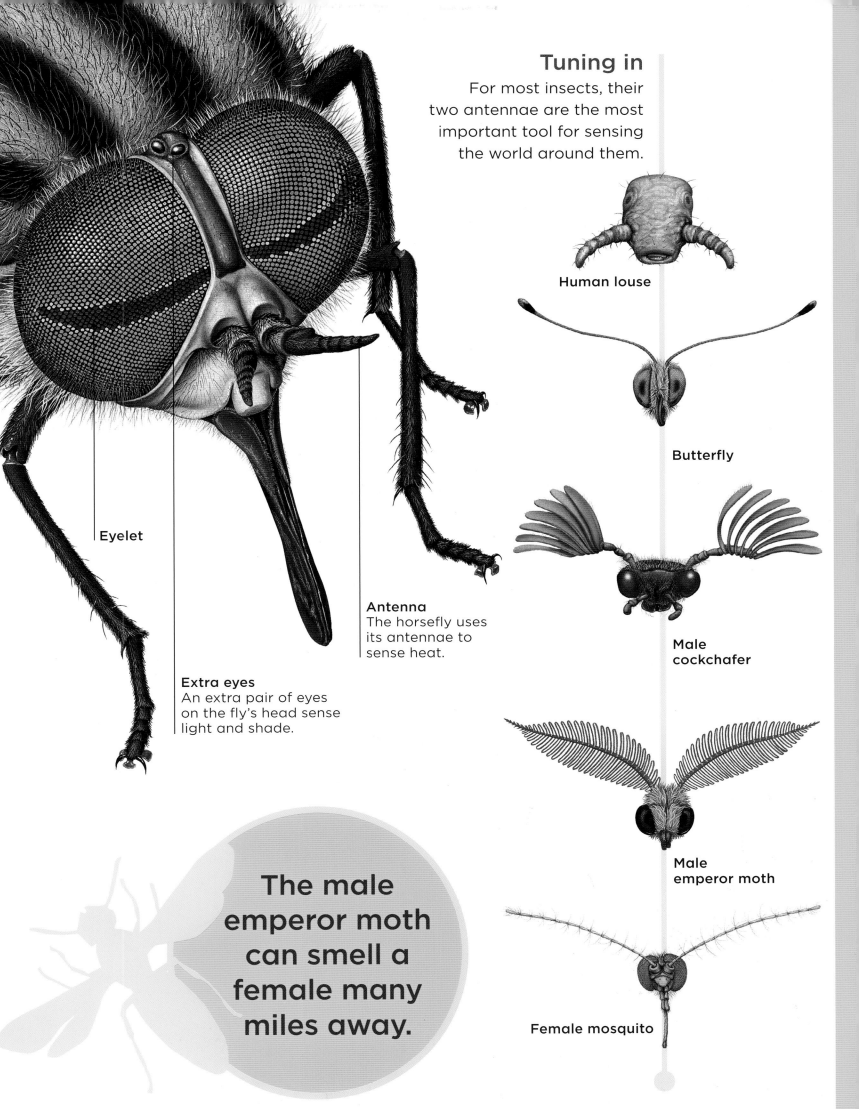

Eyelet

Extra eyes
An extra pair of eyes on the fly's head sense light and shade.

Antenna
The horsefly uses its antennae to sense heat.

Tuning in
For most insects, their two antennae are the most important tool for sensing the world around them.

Human louse

Butterfly

Male cockchafer

Male emperor moth

Female mosquito

The male emperor moth can smell a female many miles away.

Finding food

Insects spend most of their lives finding and eating food. Some insects eat plants. Some insects eat other animals. Others eat a bit of both. A few insects even survive by drinking blood!

The red coloring used in some foods is made from crushed beetles.

Meat eater
This praying mantis uses its fast front legs to catch insects to eat.

Praying mantis

Butterfly

Hickory horned
devil caterpillar

Plant eater
This caterpillar has strong
jaws to chew through its
favorite food of tough leaves.

29

Changing forms

Some insect babies are called nymphs. Nymphs look like small adults, without the wings. Other insect babies are called larvae. Larvae look very different from their parents. Both nymphs and larvae grow out of their young bodies and change into adults.

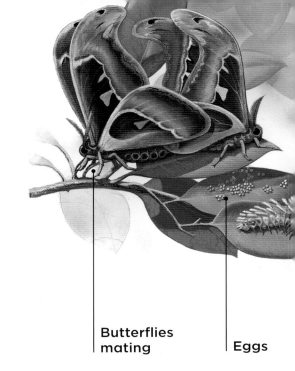

Butterflies mating

Eggs

Growing larger

A baby cicada is called a nymph. As the nymph gets older, it sheds its outer shell to make room for its growing body.

INSIDER

A bee starts life as a larva. It grows inside its waxy cell. While it grows, other bees bring it food to eat. Soon it will turn into an adult bee.

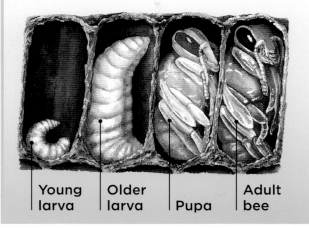

Young larva

Older larva

Pupa

Adult bee

Water baby

Dragonflies start life underwater. A dragonfly nymph can live underwater for five years. As it grows larger, it sheds its skin. When it is fully grown, it crawls out of the water and flies away.

Dragonfly laying eggs

Eggs

All change

A butterfly starts life as an egg, which grows into a larva. Butterfly larvae are called caterpillars. After a few weeks, the caterpillar's skin changes and it turns into a pupa. The adult butterfly forms inside the pupa. Once it is ready, the butterfly breaks out of its case and flies away.

Caterpillar

Pupa

Adult butterfly

Dragonflies mating

Nymph

Crawling out of its shell

Adult dragonfly

Spiders

There are more than 35,000 kinds of spiders. They are different from insects because they move on eight legs instead of six. They also have bodies that are divided into two parts. Lots of people are afraid of them, but most spiders are harmless to you and me.

Leg
All spiders have eight legs.

Claw
Claws help spiders cling to webs and rough ground.

Pedipalp
Spiders use pedipalps to touch and taste.

SPIDER EYES

You can tell a lot about a spider by its eyes.

Ogre-faced spider
This spider has huge eyes that it uses to hunt in the dark.

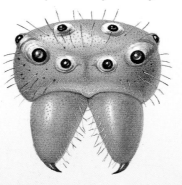

Crab spider
The crab spider has good eyes for seeing prey that is close by.

Huntsman spider
This spider has spread-out eyes that are good for hunting.

Woodlouse-eating spider
This spider has to use its sense of touch to find prey because its eyes are very small.

Eye
Most spiders
have eight eyes.

Most spiders smell through special hairs on the tips of their legs.

Fang
Spider fangs
stick out from
their jaws.

Jaws

Some spiders have fangs
that swing from side to
side. Others have fangs
that move up and down.
Both kinds of fangs are
good for catching prey.

Spider body

Most spiders are similar in shape,
but they do come in many sizes.
The smallest spider is the size of
a pinhead. The largest is the size
of a dinner plate.

Side-to-side

Up-and-down

Web spinners

Some spiders catch their food in a web. Most strands of the web are strong and sticky. Unlucky insects that fly into the web get stuck in these strands and cannot escape. The spider wraps them in more strands until it is ready to eat.

Silk strands

Spiders make their webs from silk. They know when something has landed on the web because they can feel the strands move.

Tightrope

Some strands of the spider web are not sticky. The spider uses these strands to walk on.

Non-sticky

These strands run out from the center of the web.

Sticky

These strands run around the web.

African signature spider

Silk

The spider's silk is squeezed out from here.

Redback spider

The strands of a spider's web are easy to see when covered in morning dew.

FANCY FEET

Spiders that build webs have three claws on each foot. The claws hook on to the strands of the web.

Claw

Hunting spiders

Spiders that do not build webs to catch their food are called hunting spiders. Some jump or run quickly to catch their victims. Others hide and wait for their meals to come to them.

Jumping spiders have large eyes. They can see their prey from far away.

Crab spider

Honeybee

Hide and seek

This crab spider looks like the flowers that it lives on. Insects that get too close to it are caught and eaten.

CLEVER SILK

These spiders do not build webs, but they do use silk to hunt.

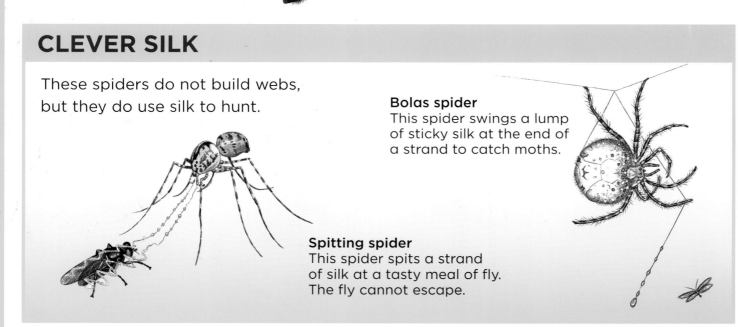

Bolas spider
This spider swings a lump of sticky silk at the end of a strand to catch moths.

Spitting spider
This spider spits a strand of silk at a tasty meal of fly. The fly cannot escape.

Needle fangs

The Sydney funnel-web spider has large fangs. It uses them to inject venom into its victim. The venom stops the victim moving and makes it easier for the spider to eat.

Large fang

Venom

In position
The spider raises its fangs, ready to strike.

Leg
This spider balances on its four back legs as it lifts up its fangs.

Tarantulas can eat mice, frogs, and small birds.

Spider survival

Many animals, including birds, frogs, and some insects, like to make a meal of spiders. Luckily, spiders have lots of ways to avoid being eaten. If hiding or running away does not work, then they may have to fight back.

Big and hairy

Some tarantulas flick their body hairs at their attackers. The hairs stick in the skin and are itchy and painful. Other tarantulas make a hissing sound to scare enemies away.

ROLL UP

Namib wheel spiders can curl up their legs and roll away from any danger.

Attack
This wheel spider is being attacked by a wasp . . .

Getaway
. . . so it curls up into a ball and rolls away.

Spider hair

The hairs on a spider are sensitive to movement in the air and on the ground. Spiders use them to feel if an enemy is coming near.

Wasp

Trapdoor spider

Bottoms up

This trapdoor spider blocks its burrow with its own backside to avoid being stung by a wasp. The wasp's stinger cannot break through the thick skin.

Some spiders will shed a leg to escape from an attacker.

Showing off

Spiders use smell, sight, touch, hearing, and taste to defend themselves, catch food, and find out what is happening in the world around them. Spiders also use senses to understand other spiders and to find mates.

Body talk

Jumping spiders do a special dance when they are getting to know each other. The male waves his legs in the air to attract the female and to show off his bright colors.

Female spider

Large eyes
A jumping spider can easily spot a mate with its large eyes.

Male spider

Some female spiders eat the male spider after they mate.

Water way

This male raft spider sends out ripples across the water to let females know he is around.

CAREFUL APPROACH

The male signature spider plucks the strands of the female's web in a special way. She then knows he is a mate and not a meal.

Male

Female

41

Spider life

Every spider starts life as an egg. Most mother spiders wrap their eggs in silk to protect them. When they are born, baby spiders look like tiny versions of their parents. Most spiders give birth to thousands of babies, but only a few live to become adults.

ALL CHANGE

Spiders have to shed their skin as they grow. They usually stop shedding their skin when they become adults.

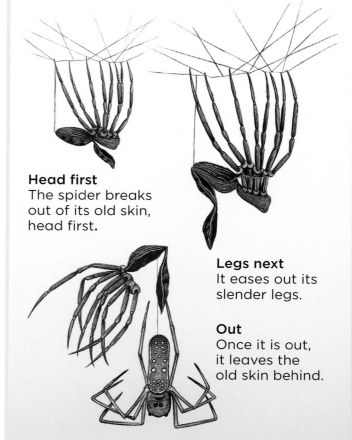

Head first
The spider breaks out of its old skin, head first.

Legs next
It eases out its slender legs.

Out
Once it is out, it leaves the old skin behind.

Good mother
The nursery-web spider uses silk to make a safe nest for her babies to live in. She also stays close to protect them.

Mother spider

Baby carrier
Wolf spider babies cling to their mother's body after being born.

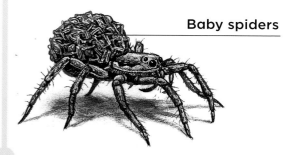

Baby spiders

Time to fly

Some baby spiders leave their nest by flying through the air on tiny threads of silk. This is called ballooning. The wind carries them to a new place to live.

Baby spider

Spider relatives

Scorpions, mites, and ticks are close relatives of spiders. Like spiders, they all have eight legs. Scorpions can deliver a nasty sting, but most are harmless to humans. Ticks and mites are small and often live on other animals.

Some scorpions are so large that they can eat frogs.

Night glow
All scorpions glow in the dark under special types of light. No one is sure why.

POWERFUL JAWS

This wind scorpion has very powerful jaws, which it uses to catch prey.

Getting close

Scorpions use their tails to kill their prey and to fight off enemies. These scorpions are dancing together before mating. They grab each other's pincers and hold their tails high in the air.

Ticks and mites

Ticks drink blood. Most mites are so small you can see them only with a microscope.

Tick

Velvet mite

Stinger
Poison comes out of the stinger on the end of the scorpion's tail.

Glossary

Tarantula

Ladybug

antennae
The long growths on the heads of insects, which they use to sense the world around them

aphids
A group of small insects that suck up plant juices

attacker
An insect or spider that tries to hurt another

creatures
All living insects and animals, other than human beings

defend
To protect from danger or attack

delicate
Very fine in texture, such as a spider's web

deliver
To give to another

dew
Drops of moisture

digesting
Breaking up food so that it can be absorbed into the body

direction
The point toward which something moves

enemies
Groups of bugs that are violent toward other groups of bugs

eyelets
The many tiny eyes that make up some insects' eyes

fangs
Long, pointed growths, similar to teeth

inject
To insert fluid into the body of another, such as a spider injecting venom into its prey

joints
Places where two or more body parts join

Yellow emperor moth

European wasp

larva
A baby insect that looks different from its parents

nectar
A sugary substance that insects eat

nymph
A baby insect that can sometimes look similar to its parents

prey
Any insect or bug hunted or killed by another insect or bug

pupa
The stage between larva and adult in some insects

scales
Thin, flat pieces forming the skin that covers a butterfly's wings

senses
The powers of sight, hearing, smell, taste, and touch

strands
Single threads, such as those that make up a spider's web

survive
To continue to live

threatened
The possibility that one may be hurt

tilt
To be in a sloping position

venom
A poison used by stinging or biting insects

victim
A bug that suffers injury or death

Index

Credits

Key t=top; l=left; r=right; tl=top left; tcl=top center left; tc=top center; tcr=top center right; tr=top right; cl=center left; c=center; cr=center right; b=bottom; bl=bottom left; bcl=bottom center left; bc=bottom center; bcr=bottom center right; br=bottom right

Photographs
COR=Corel Corp.; GI=Getty Images; iS=istockphotocom; PD=Photodisc; PL=photolibrary.com
8bl PL; **11**tr PL; **12**bl COR; **16**cl iS **22**tr iS; **26**cl PL; **35**tr PD; **36**tr GI; **38**br PL tr PD; **41**bl PL; **44**cl PL

Illustrations
Front cover Sandra Doyle/The Art Agency tr, Christer Eriksson c, Ray Grinaway br, David Kirshner tl
Back cover David Kirshner tr Rob Mancini br

Susanna Addario **20**c; Anne Bowman **11**br; Sandra Doyle/The Art Agency **9**tr, **12**c cr, **25**t, **32**bl, **40**c, **41**br; Simone End **1**c, **14**tr, **25**b; Christer Eriksson **6**c, **10**c, **14**c, **24**c, **28**c, **44**cr; Alan Ewart **36**c; Giuliano Fornari **35**bl; Jon Gittoes **38**bl; Ray Grinaway **6**bl cl, **16**bl c, **19**cr, **24**bl, **36**bl cl, **42**bl tr; Tim Hayward/Bernard Thornton Artists UK **6**bl, **42**br, **43**c; Ian Jackson/ The Art Agency **5**tr, **11**br, **17**tr; Cathy Johnson **10**c; Janet Jones **45**tr; David Kirshner **6**bl, **8**c; Frank

Knight **30**t; Rob Mancini **3**c, **18**bl cl, **19**br, **33**br, **34**bl **44**bl, **45**tr; James McKinnon **12**tr, **39**c; Edwina Riddell **30**bl; Steve Roberts/The Art Agency **15**br, **24**br, **29**c; Trevor Ruth **17**b, **19**bl c; Claudia Saraceni **16**bl; Chris Shields/The Art Agency **22**cl, **26**bl, **36**bl; Kevin Stead **4**c, **9**br cr, **20**bl t, **22**c, **23**tl, **26**t, **27**r, **30**b, **34**c; Thomas Trojer **32**c